MEGA TRACTORS

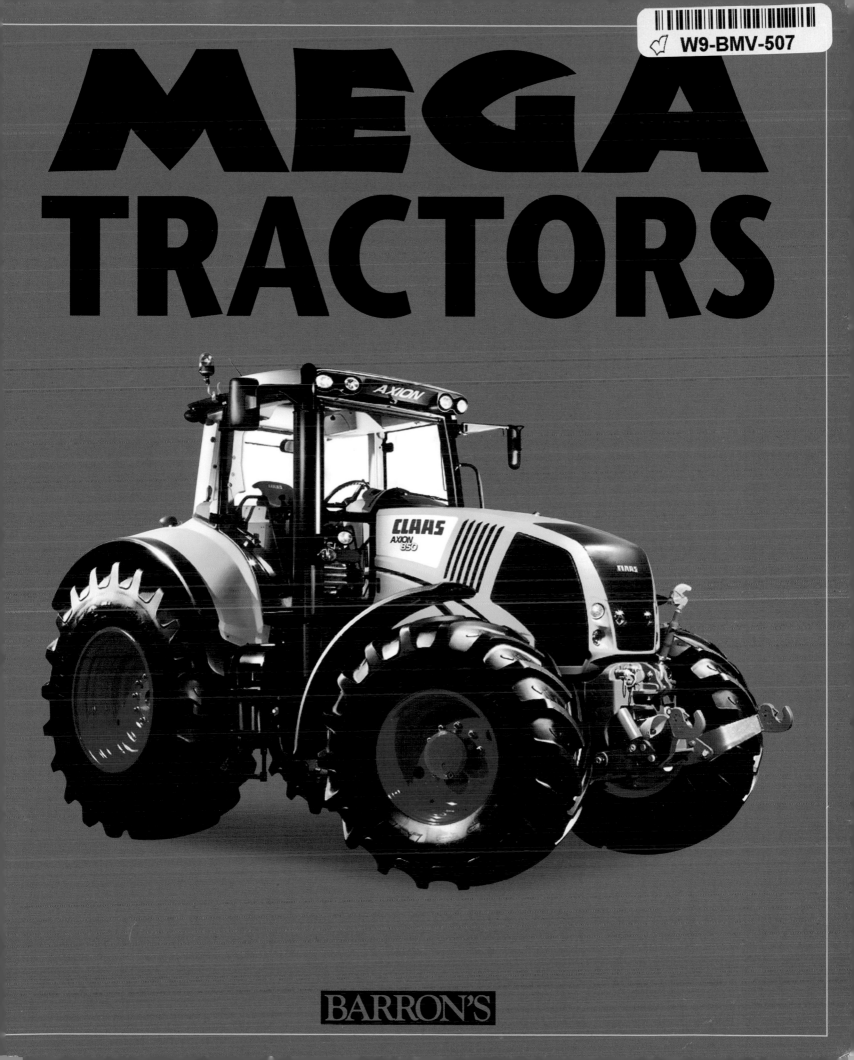

BARRON'S

First edition for the United States and Canada published in 2016
by Barron's Educational Series, Inc.
Copyright © 2008, 2014 by Picthall and Gunzi,
An imprint of Award Publications Limited, The Old Riding School,
The Welbeck Estate, Worksop, S80 3LR

Designer: Paul Calver
Written and edited by: Louise Pritchard and Christiane Gunzi
Editorial assistant: Katy Rayner
Consultant: Peter Love

All inquiries should be addressed to:
Barron's Educational Series, Inc.
250 Wireless Boulevard, Hauppauge, New York 11788
www.barronseduc.com

Thank you to the following companies and individuals for the use of their images: AGCO
Audio Visual Department; Bargam SPA; Case IH; Christian Brocks – European Tractor
Pulling Committee; Claas; Clarke Machinery Group Ltd; Clayton Engineering Ltd; Don
Carter of Oxbo International Corporation; Horsch Maschinen GmbH; Iain Hawkins with
"Wicked" at STPC Finals 2006, by Lynn Hawkins; Kubota (U.K.) Limited; Kverneland Group;
New Holland; Peter Love; Scottish Tractor Pullers Club; Tonutti Spa; TYM International Ltd;
www.cfgphoto.com; www.tractorpulling.com

Please note that every effort has been made to check the accuracy of the information
contained in this book, and to credit the copyright holders correctly. Picthall and Gunzi
apologize for any unintentional errors or omissions, and would be happy to include
revisions to content and/or acknowledgements in subsequent editions of this book.

ISBN: 978-1-4380-0917-9
Library of Congress Control No.: 2016933264

Manufactured by: Dream Colour (Hong Kong) Printing Ltd., Foshan, China

Date of Manufacture: June 2016

Printed in China

9 8 7 6 5 4 3 2 1

CONTENTS

Farm Tractors 4

Combine Harvesters 14

Loaders and Lifters 24

Crawler Tractors 6

Vegetable Harvesters 16

Rescue Tractors 26

Old Tractors 8

Balers 18

Road Builders 28

Tractors and Plows 10

Foragers 20

Racing Tractors 30

Crop Sprayers 12

Giant Tractors 22

Let's Match! 32

rARM TRACTORS

Every farm has a tractor. Most tractors have big wheels and tires so they can drive across fields as well as on roads. Tractors are powerful vehicles. They can pull and push other machines and trailers around the farm.

Massey Ferguson tractor

Massey Ferguson

This Massey Ferguson has a low roof, so it can drive inside barns and buildings. Tractors have lots of gears and can go fast or slow.

Can you point to?

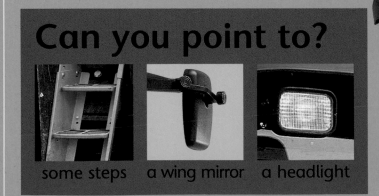

some steps   a wing mirror   a headlight

John Deere

John Deere tractors are always green and yellow. They have been painted this color since 1918.

John Deere tractor

What color is the Massey Ferguson?

New Holland tractor

New Holland

This tractor can almost drive itself. A computer inside remembers what the driver did and tells the tractor to do it again, at the touch of a button.

CRAWLER TRACTORS

A crawler tractor moves along on rubber tracks wrapped around small wheels. The tracks do not squash the soil as much as normal wheels do, so crawler tractors are useful for working on soft, muddy ground.

Can you point to?

an exhaust

two wheels

a light

Quadtrac tractor

This red tractor has four tracks. There are two at the front and two at the back. These tracks make the tractor easier to turn. The word "quad" means four.

What are this crawler's tracks made of?

Case Quadtrac

Rubber tracks

Steering
wheel

Exhaust

Caterpillar
crawler
tractor

Caterpillar crawler

The machines made by Caterpillar are
named after a caterpillar because the
crawler tracks move like creepy crawlies!

CASE IH

QUADTRAC

680

CASE IH

OLD TRACTORS

The first farm tractors with engines were made about 140 years ago. They were powered by steam. Lots of old tractors still work today, and people take them to tractor shows.

Fordson tractor

This Fordson tractor was made in London over 60 years ago. Its top speed was less than 7 miles an hour!

Massey Ferguson 188

Winning prizes

People who own classic old tractors polish them and take care of them well. They often enter their tractors in competitions. This Massey Ferguson is about 40 years old.

Which tractor is blue and orange?

A popular tractor

This type of John Deere tractor was first made in 1923. It was popular on farms for 30 years and it had big steel wheels.

Exhaust pipe

Tractor's name

Steel wheels

John Deere D

Fordson E27N Major

9

TRACTORS AND PLOWS

Every autumn, farmers get their fields ready for planting seeds. They use a tractor to pull or push a plow over the fields. The plow turns the soil over so it is ready for planting crops.

Can you point to?

some numbers   a circle   some letters

John Deere tractor plowing a field

Plow ———————

Neat and tidy

Tractors use machines called seed drills to plant seeds in the ground. The seed drills plant the seeds in straight rows.

Can you see the yellow wheels?

Tractor planting with a seed drill

Heavy work

This tractor has four-wheel drive. The power goes to all four wheels so that they grip the ground and help the tractor pull the plow along.

Massey Ferguson tractor plowing

MASSEY FERGUSON

4435

CROP SPRAYERS

Farmers use a machine called a sprayer to spray their crops with a special liquid to keep insects away. The liquid is stored in a big tank. The spray comes out of a long arm, called a boom.

Can you point to?

some stripes   a ladder   a logo

No help needed

This Bargam Mac sprayer is high up off the ground. It has narrow wheels so it does not damage the crops. It sprays as it moves along, and it can carry 1,057 gallons (4,000 liters) of liquid in its tank.

Driver's cab

Safety rail

Spray

Boom

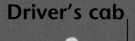

Folded away

This yellow crop sprayer needs a tractor to pull it along. When the sprayer is not being used the boom folds up like wings. It is called a gullwing boom.

John Deere tractor pulling a sprayer along

Tank

Where does all the spray come out?

4000 s

Bargam Mac sprayer working in the fields

COMBINE HARVESTERS

Huge combine harvesters cut the crops of wheat and barley. They separate the stalks from the grains. They put the grains in the grain tank and leave the stalks on the ground. All the stalks dry in the sun and turn into straw!

Grain tank

Claas Lexion combine harvester cutting crops

Ladder

LEXION 600

CLAAS

20

Teamwork

A Claas Lexion uses its cutter bar to cut a strip 30 feet (9 meters) wide. On very large farms these machines sometimes work in teams.

Where does the harvester put the grain?

Three combine harvesters at work

Claas Lexion

This is one of the biggest, most popular combine harvesters in the world. It can cut 320,000 pounds (160 tons) of grain and straw in one hour!

Cutter bar

VEGETABLE HARVESTERS

Some harvesters collect potatoes, sweet corn, and other vegetables. They cut down the vegetables, then separate them from the stalks and leaves, and put them into a big tank on the back.

Can you point to?

a container   a filter   a rectangle

Where can you see a green trailer?

Driver

Oxbo harvester

Cutting sweet corn

This yellow Oxbo harvester travels from field to field like a tractor. Farmers often use these machines to do just one kind of job. This one is collecting sweet corn.

16

Sugar beet

This red harvester is collecting sugar beet. It puts the beets in the tank. When the tank is full, they go into a trailer on the tractor. The tractor will take them away.

Tank

BALERS

Machines called balers collect straw left on the ground after harvesting. Then the balers turn the straw into round or square bales. One baler can pick up the straw, roll it into a bale, wrap it, and drop it in the field to be collected later.

Wrapping the bales

This tractor has a special machine on the back that wraps up round bales in plastic to keep them dry.

New Holland tractor pulling a square baler

Straw roll

This Massey Ferguson tractor is pulling a round baler. The baler makes a bale, then rolls it out of the back. The driver must be careful because the straw bale could roll down a hill!

Massey Ferguson baler making bales

How many bales of straw can you count?

Flat sides

This New Holland baler makes big square bales. The bales are really rectangular, but they are called square. Square bales are easy to stack because they have flat sides.

FORAGERS

Machines called foragers cut up grass and other plants to make forage. Forage is a name for the dry stems and leaves that horses and cows eat in winter.

Where is the red tractor?

Claas Jaguar forager

Big jaguar

This Claas Jaguar cuts the plants and chops the stems. It pours the bits through a chute into a trailer on the back of a tractor.

Chute

Forage _____

Trailer

Making hay

This tractor is pulling a rake. The rake's wheels have spikes that turn the grass and help it dry into hay.

GIANT TRACTOR

This is the world's biggest farm tractor. It was built over 30 years ago and works in the USA. Its tank holds 1,000 gallons (3,785 liters) of fuel. That's about 1,000 times more than a car's tank can hold!

Wow!

The boy below is three years old. See how tiny he is next to this tractor!

What is this mega tractor called?

Larger than life

This tractor's name is "Big Bud." It is just over 14 feet (4 meters) tall and weighs more than 90,000 pounds (45 tons). It has eight tires and each one is 8 feet (2.4 meters) high, taller than a full-grown man.

LOADERS AND LIFTERS

Some modern tractors have an arm with a bucket or fork on the end for lifting things. These are very useful on farms because there are lots of things that need lifting.

Caterpillar lifting straw bales

Safety frame

Driving seat

Trac-Lift TM T450

Little digger

This red tractor is from Japan. It has a small digger bucket on the front for lifting soil, sand, and other light things.

Tight fit

The tractor below is easy to drive around and can get into small spaces! Its bucket is useful for lifting animal food and bedding.

Kubota tractor

Bucket

Which of these tractors is made in Japan?

Fork

Lifting arm

DIECI

Lifting fork

This yellow tractor has an arm like a fork-lift truck's arm. The fork on the end can lift and carry big bales of hay or straw.

RESCUE TRACTORS

Special tractors help to put boats in the sea and take them out again. This Talus sea tractor was specially made to work with the RNLI lifeboats on beaches. It is waterproof so its engine and electronics can work in the sea.

Roof hatch

Cab door

Working in water

The Talus tractor can drive in up to 5 feet (1.6 meters) of water. If it broke down in the sea, it could be left on the seabed without any water getting in!

Can you point to?

a flag   a grill   a lock

Tractor on tracks

A crawler tractor is useful on sandy beaches because it does not get stuck. The tractor uses a winch to put the boat on a trailer, then pulls it to the boathouse.

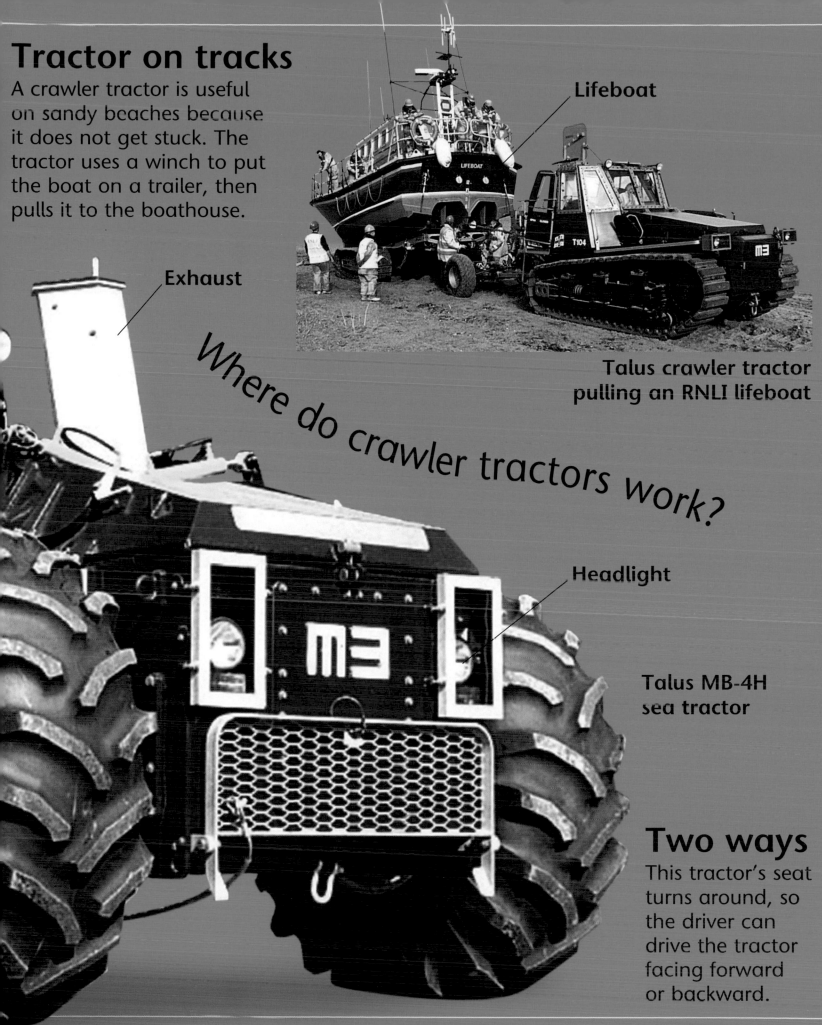

Lifeboat

Exhaust

Talus crawler tractor pulling an RNLI lifeboat

Where do crawler tractors work?

Headlight

Talus MB-4H sea tractor

Two ways

This tractor's seat turns around, so the driver can drive the tractor facing forward or backward.

ROAD BUILDERS

Big, powerful tractors help with road works, where they do many different jobs. They pull heavy containers and machines and help to dig and lay new road surfaces.

Wing mirror

Grill

Working together

These tractors are making a new road. One tractor is laying down the surface. The other one makes sure the road is level.

What is this big tractor pulling?

Light

Can you point to?

a tube

a triangle

a rectangle

Cement carrier

MP & KM GOLDING

www.roadreclamation.co.uk

Tel:

Steps

Fendt tractor pulling
a cement carrier

Carrying cement

This tractor is pulling a cement
carrier. The driver moves a stick
called a joystick to make the
tractor go faster or slower, and
forward or backward.

RACING TRACTORS

Some amazing tractors enter competitions called "tractor pulling." They have to pull a special type of sled along, which gets heavier the farther it is pulled. The tractor that pulls the sled the farthest is the winner.

Roll cage

Exhaust pipe

"Rocky" racing tractor

Sled

"Wicked" racing tractor

Noise and dirt

The tractors make lots of smoke and noise and spray dirt everywhere! Some tractors have extra-large wheels to help them to grip. Others have turbo-charged engines.

What is the driver wearing?

Extra weight

Doing wheelies

Tractors sometimes do "wheelies," when the two front wheels come off the ground. They have weights to stop them from flipping over.

Can you point to?

checkerboard   a driver   a wheel

LET'S MATCH!

Can you find all the matching pairs on this page?

Where are all the blue tractors?

TRACKS

TIRES

LIGHTS

TIRE

TRACKS

LIGHTS